Smithsonian

# HOW TO DRAW
# INCREDIBLE
# OCEAN ANIMALS

WRITTEN BY KRISTEN MCCURRY
ILLUSTRATED BY JARED OSTERHOLD

CAPSTONE PRESS
a capstone imprint

# TABLE OF CONTENTS

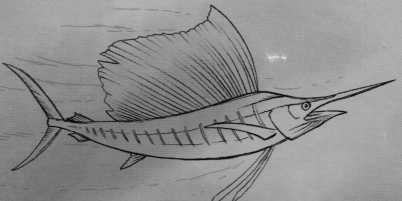

# ANEMONEFISH

STEP 1

STEP 2

STEP 3

4

You may know them as clownfish. Also called anemonefish, these fish are named for the poisonous sea anemones they live in. Even though they are covered with a layer of mucus, the anemonefish must get used to the anemone's sting. They do this by lightly touching parts of their bodies to the anemones before moving in.

STEP 4

FINISHED!

# ATLANTIC BLUE MARLIN

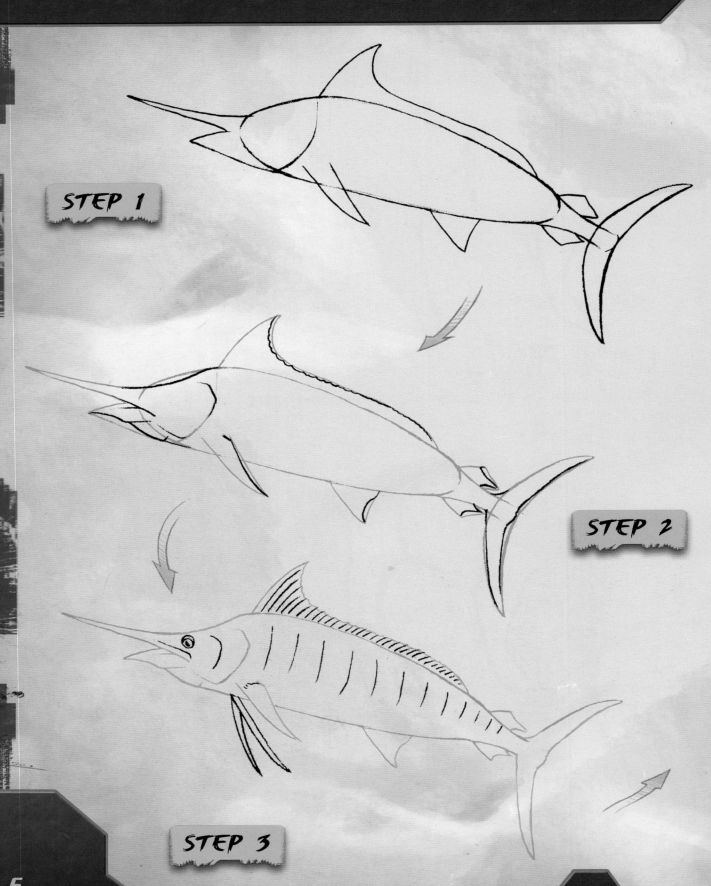

STEP 1

STEP 2

STEP 3

The blue marlin is one of the biggest fish in the ocean. The females weigh more than 1,800 pounds (817 kilograms)! This beautiful large fish is also known for the long, pointy spear coming off its nose. The marlin uses its spear to kill prey as it slices through schools of fish.

**STEP 4**

**FINISHED!**

STEP 1

STEP 2

STEP 3

These giant, speedy fish travel many miles as they zip between cold and tropical waters. Bluefin tuna can pull their retractable fins in close to their bodies to go even faster—up to 43 miles (69 kilometers) per hour. Bluefin tuna are warm-blooded, which is unusual among fish.

## STEP 4

## FINISHED!

# BLUE WHALE

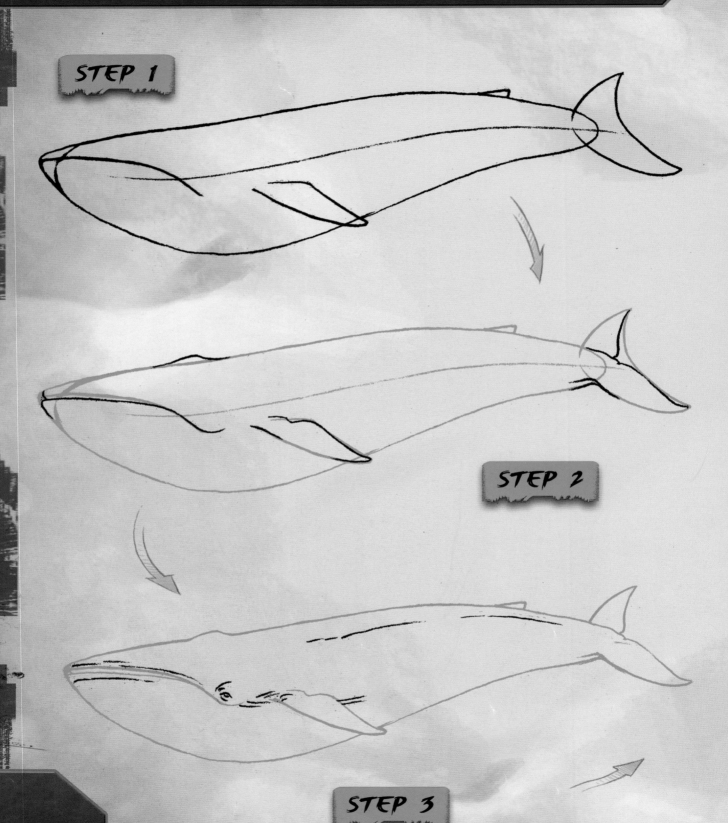

STEP 1

STEP 2

STEP 3

Blue whales are famous for being the largest animals on Earth—ever. At 100 feet (30 meters) they are as long as three school buses! What's it take to feed an animal that big? Tons of food—literally. Each day an adult male eats up to 4 tons (3.6 metric tons) of tiny shrimplike creatures called krill.

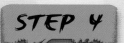

**STEP 4**

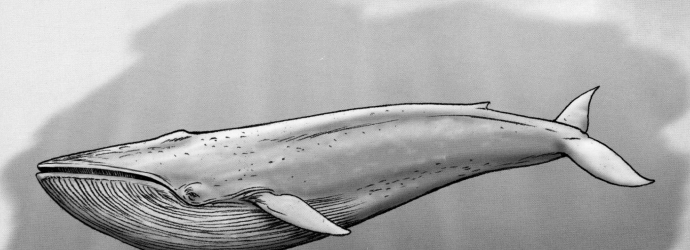

**FINISHED!**

STEP 1

STEP 2

STEP 3

Bottlenose dolphins are social animals that live in groups. They team up to hunt too. One trick is to surround a school of fish and then take turns feeding from the clustered prey. Bottlenose dolphins are graceful swimmers and have been known to jump as high as 16 feet (4.9 m) out of the water. They sometimes "surf" in the wakes created by boats.

STEP 4

FINISHED!

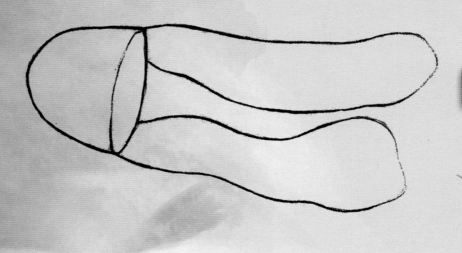

STEP 1

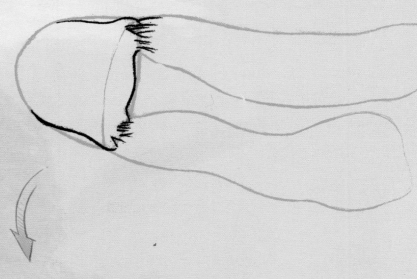

STEP 2

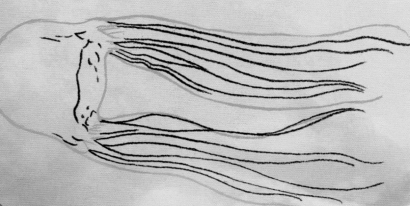

STEP 3

The box jellyfish is a beautiful creature with a deadly defense. Its venom is among the most dangerous in the world. Also known as sea wasps or marine stingers, these jellies have as many as 60 tentacles, each up to 10 feet (3 m) long. Instead of simply drifting as other jellies do, box jellyfish can actively swim.

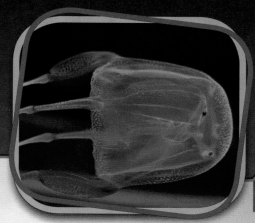

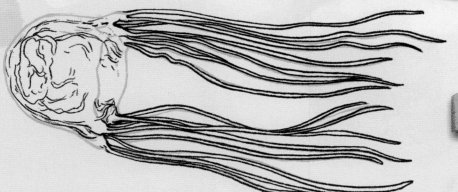

**STEP 4**

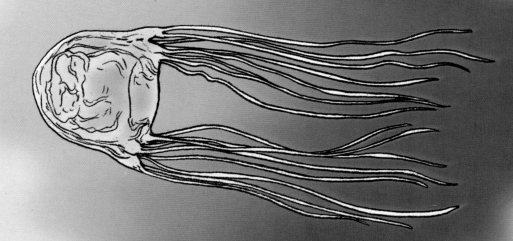

**FINISHED!**

# COELACANTH

Once thought to have gone extinct with the dinosaurs, the coelacanth, pronounced SEEL-uh-kanth, is an ancient fish. Fossils show that it has been living on Earth for more than 360 million years. This "living fossil" is more than 6 feet (1.8 m) long. It has fins on both sides of its body that stick out like legs, which it paddles as it swims.

STEP 4

FINISHED!

# DEEP SEA ANGLERFISH

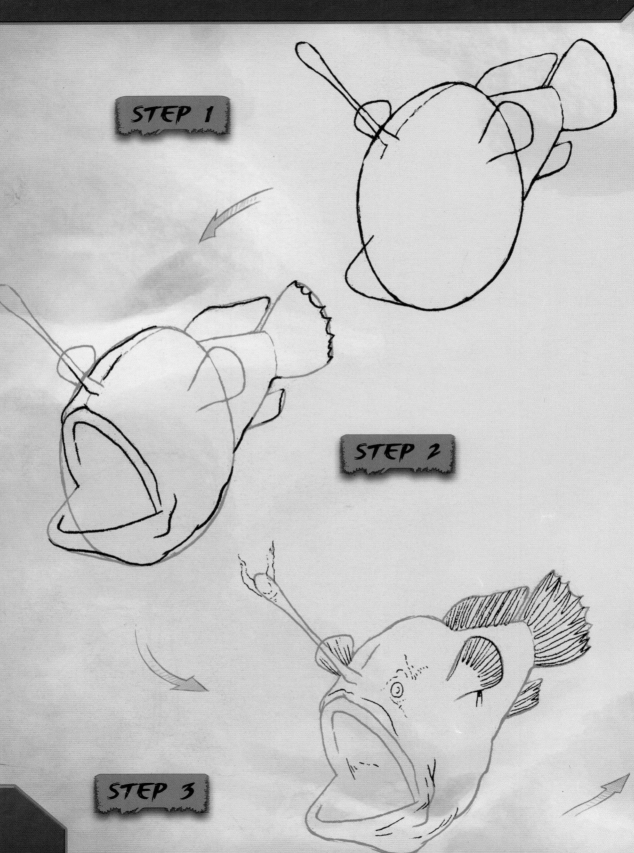

STEP 1

STEP 2

STEP 3

The female deep sea anglerfish is a small but fierce-looking creature that lurks in dark depths of the oceans. It "fishes" for its prey with a glowing fleshy spine that extends from the top of its head. The anglerfish clamps its sharp teeth down on any fish that gets too close. Its flexible jaw and body allow it to eat creatures up to twice its size.

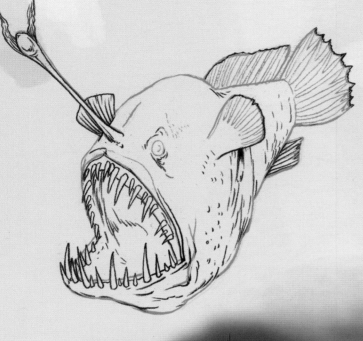

**STEP 4**

**FINISHED!**

**STEP 1**

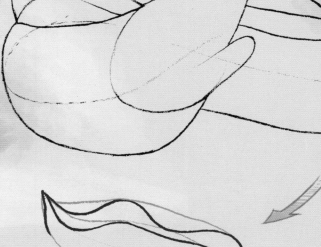

**STEP 2**

**STEP 3**

This scary-looking creature likes to hide among rocks, opening and closing its jaws as if waiting for prey. In fact, it's just breathing. Working its jaws helps keep air moving through its gills. What is frightening about this eel is its second set of jaws. They are in the eel's throat, and they work to push prey down and keep it from escaping.

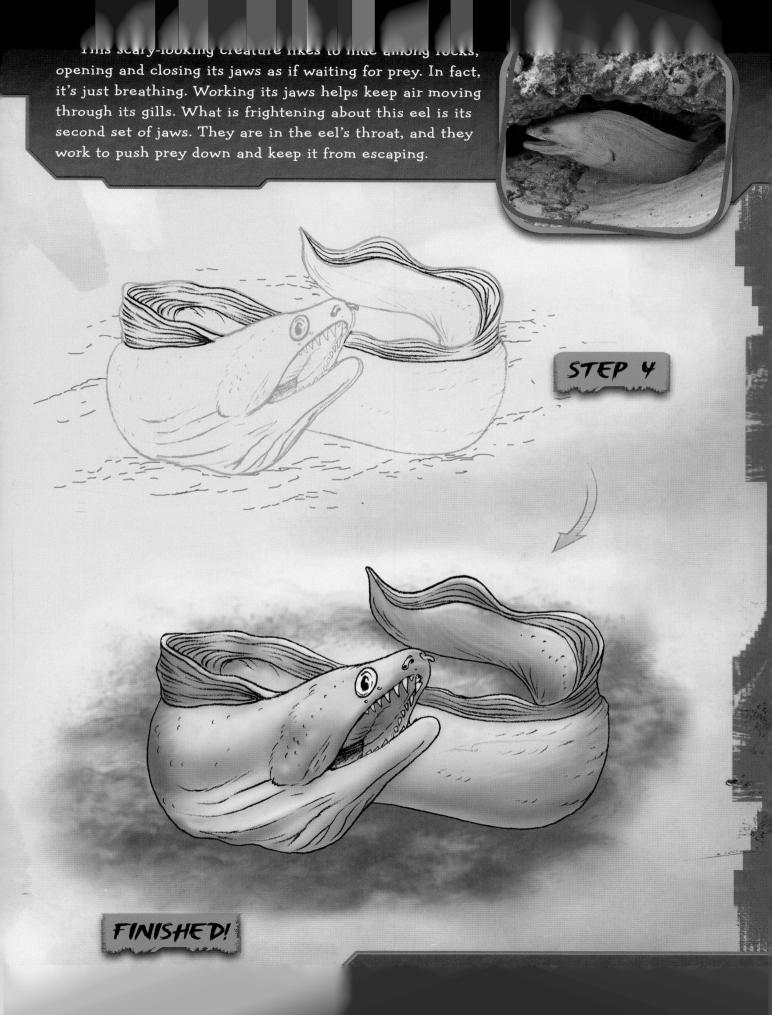

STEP 4

FINISHED!

# GIANT OCTOPUS

STEP 1

STEP 2

STEP 3

The giant octopus can grow to nearly 30 feet (9 m), but as a hatchling, this giant is only as big as a grain of rice. When defending itself, the giant octopus will squirt a cloud of ink at an attacker. The ink cloud serves as a smoke screen while the octopus makes its escape.

**STEP 4**

**FINISHED!**

STEP 1

STEP 2

STEP 3

Great whites are sleek predators that can swim up to 15 miles (24 km) per hour. These bloodhounds of the sea can sense a single drop of blood from up to 3 miles (4.8 km) away. Great white sharks are the largest predatory fish, but they don't hunt humans intentionally. They prefer sea lions, seals, and small whales.

STEP 4

FINISHED!

STEP 1

STEP 2

STEP 3

Green sea turtles are found in coastal waters all around the world, grazing on sea grasses and algae. These gentle giants may weigh more than 350 pounds (159 kg), making them the largest of the hard shell sea turtles. Mother turtles return to the same beaches where they were born to lay their eggs.

**STEP 4**

**FINISHED!**

# HAMMERHEAD SHARK

STEP 1

STEP 2

STEP 3

The odd shape of the hammerhead shark's head gives the animal an edge in hunting. With eyes on both sides of its wide face, the shark can scan a large area for prey. The hammerhead is also unusually good at detecting the electrical and chemical signals given off by prey.

STEP 4

FINISHED!

STEP 2

STEP 3

Hermit crabs are not born with their shells. After floating in the water for a while, they settle onto the bottom and must find an available snail shell. They will fight other crabs for an empty shell. Some hermit crabs stick anemones to their shells for protection. They bring the anemones with them when it is time to get a bigger shell.

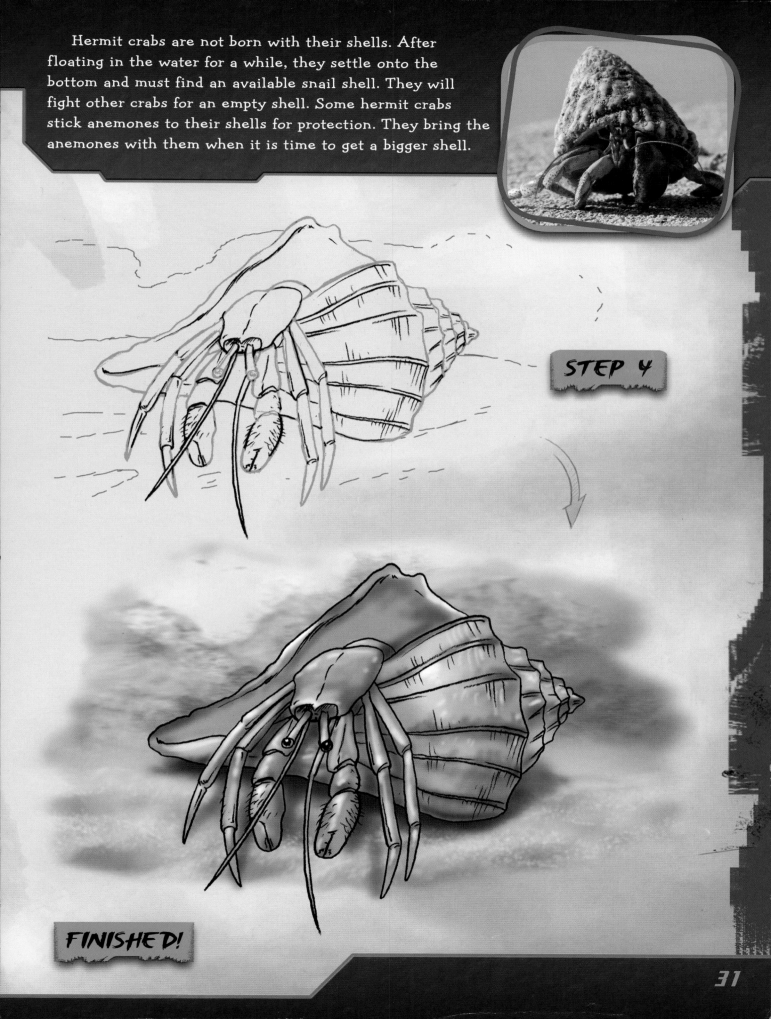

STEP 4

FINISHED!

**STEP 1**

**STEP 2**

**STEP 3**

Horseshoe crabs are relatives of spiders and scorpions. A horseshoe crab molts and sheds its shell many times as it grows. Young crabs live in shallow coastal waters, and then move into deeper waters as they get older. Horseshoe crabs come up on the beach to lay their eggs, leaving fascinating trails in the sand.

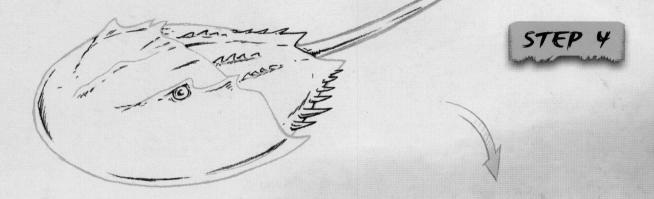

STEP 4

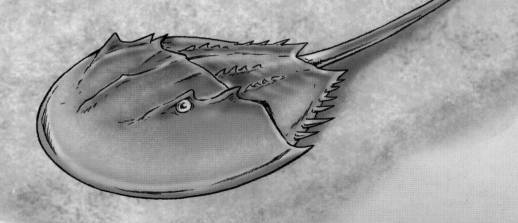

FINISHED!

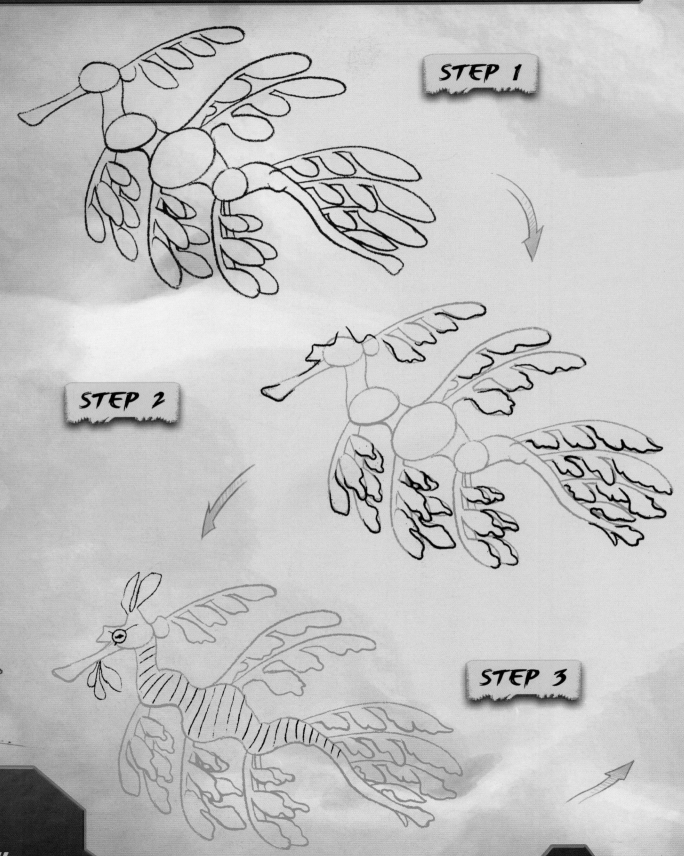

STEP 1

STEP 2

STEP 3

Plant or animal? The colorful leafy sea dragon is an animal disguised as seaweed. Sea dragons mostly drift, but they do have some ability to steer and move themselves through the Australian waters they live in. Like their sea horse cousins, sea dragon males are responsible for carrying the female's eggs.

STEP 4

FINISHED!

STEP 1

STEP 2

STEP 3

The fascinating lionfish doesn't bite, but it stings. Its pointy dorsal fins contain venom, which the fish uses to protect itself. Lionfish are popular in aquariums for their beautiful and bizarre appearance. In the Caribbean Sea, they are considered an invasive species because they have moved into this new territory and become abundant.

STEP 4

FINISHED!

STEP 1

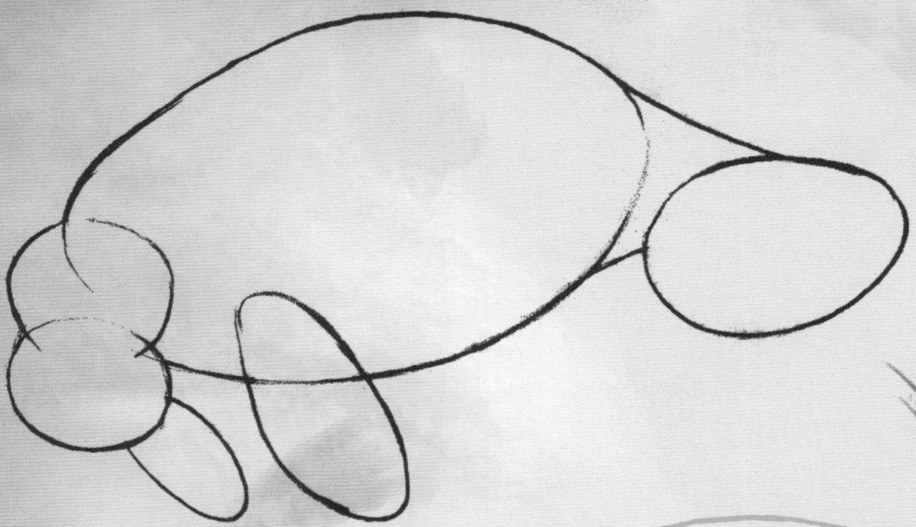

STEP 2

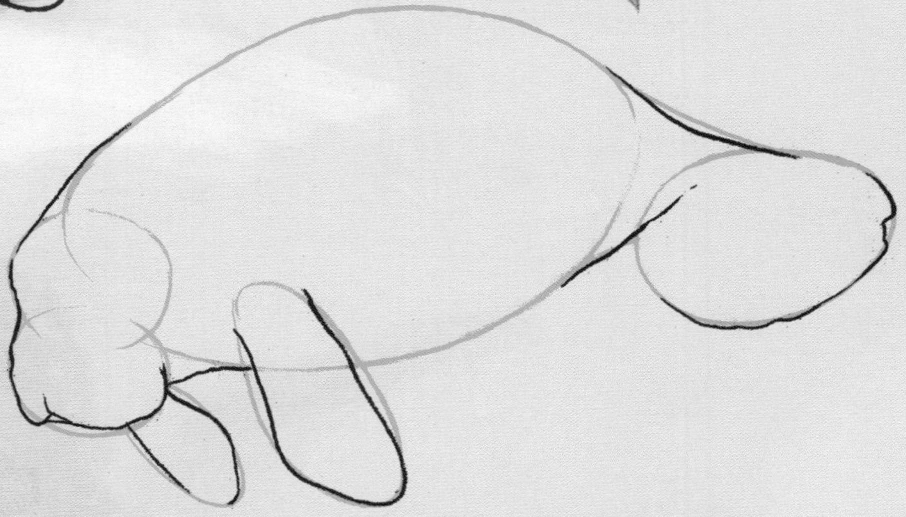

STEP 3

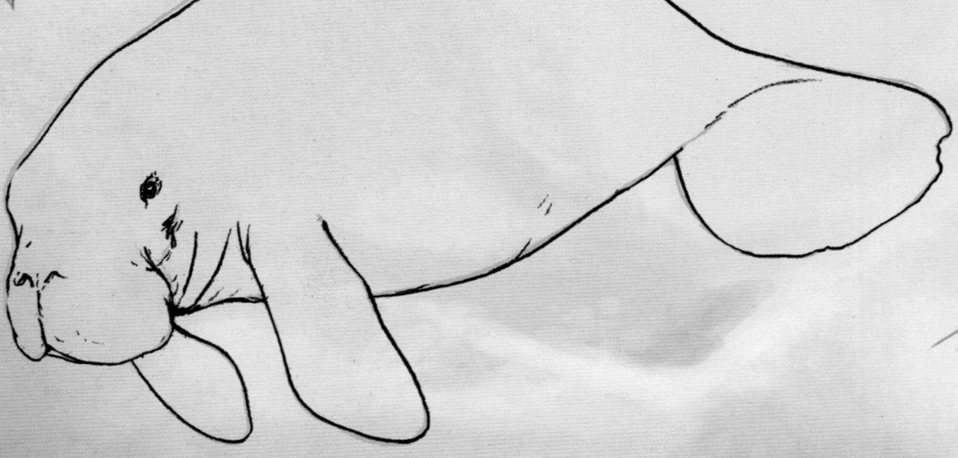

Manatees are large, slow-moving marine mammals that live in shallow coastal waters. They spend much of their time grazing on weeds and algae. Their grazing behavior has given them the nickname of "sea cow," but the manatee is most closely related to the elephant.

**STEP 4**

**FINISHED!**

STEP 1

STEP 2

STEP 3

This giant kite-shaped ray swims by flapping its fins like a bird. With fins extended, it may be 29 feet (8.8 m) wide! Because of its great size, this ray's only predators are large sharks. The manta ray lives in the reefs and lagoons of warm coastal waters. It gathers plankton and small fish into its mouth using two lobes near its face.

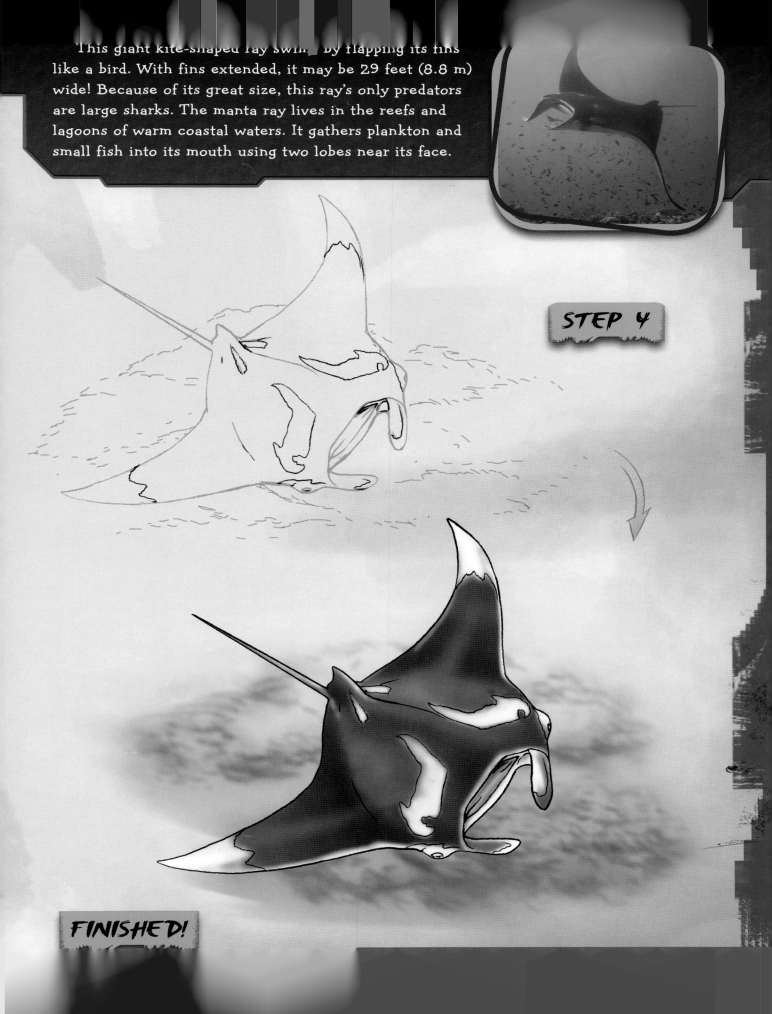

**STEP 4**

**FINISHED!**

**STEP 1**

**STEP 2**

**STEP 3**

Marine iguanas are odd-looking lizards that live only on the Galápagos Islands. These plant eaters have strong snouts and sharp teeth that they use to scrape algae off the rocks to eat. They often have white caps on their heads from sea salt they've sneezed out.

**STEP 4**

**FINISHED!**

STEP 3

The long pointy tusk of the male narwhal is actually a tooth. It can grow to nearly 9 feet (2.7 m) long. Narwhals are members of the porpoise family and dive down into deep arctic waters. These social mammals live in pods of two to 10 narwhals, but they may gather in groups of hundreds.

**STEP 4**

**FINISHED!**

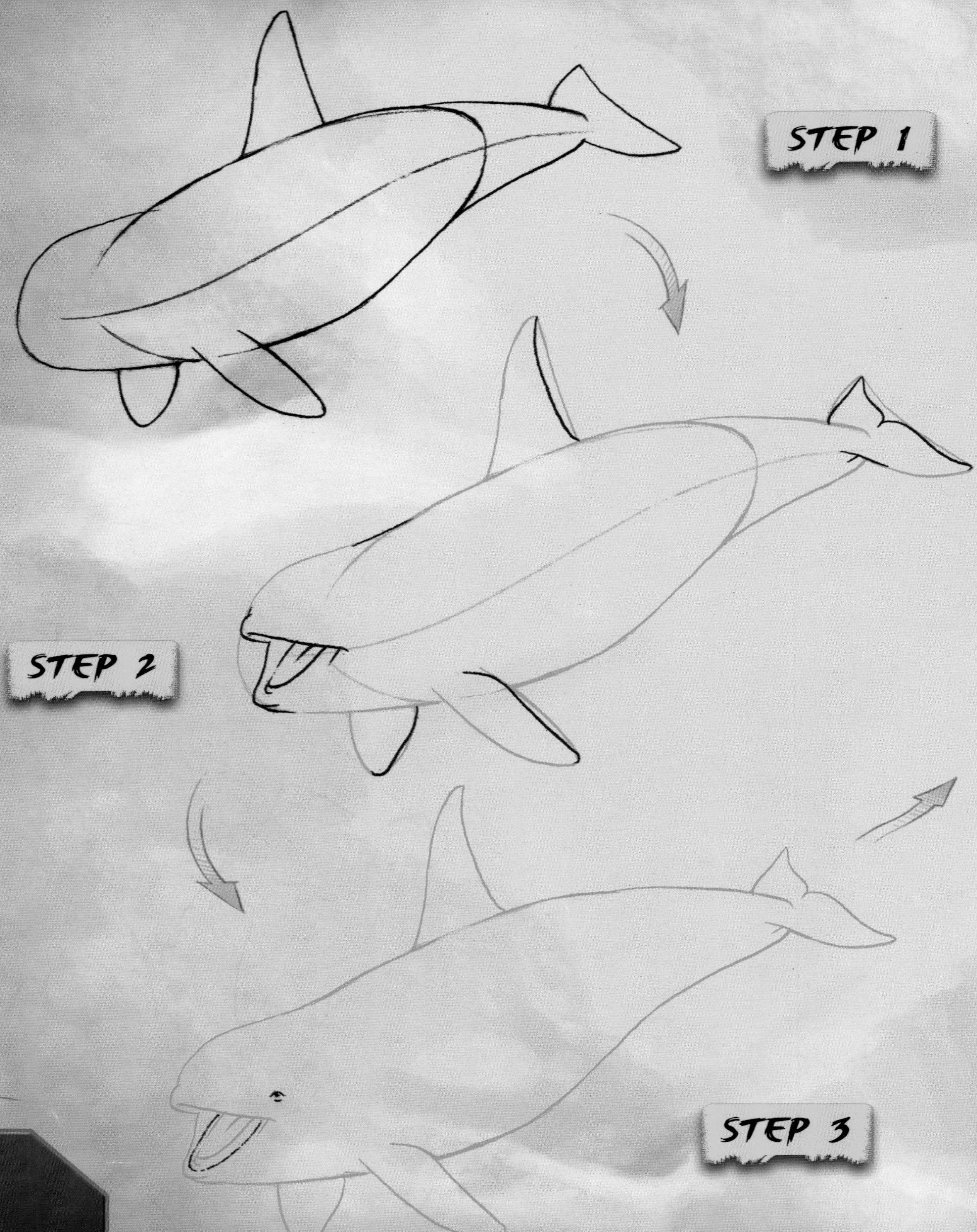
STEP 1
STEP 2
STEP 3

The orca, also known as the killer whale, is a fierce hunter. Pods of two to 15 whales hunt together to catch fish, including sharks, and marine mammals. Orcas use echolocation to locate prey—they send out clicking sounds that bounce back to let them know where animals are.

STEP 4

FINISHED!

# PORCUPINEFISH

The porcupinefish can blow itself up like a pointy balloon, using either air or water. It does this to make itself harder for predators to eat—and to scare them off. These tropical fish hide out under rocks during the day and hunt along the coral reef for sea urchins, snails, and crabs at night.

STEP 4

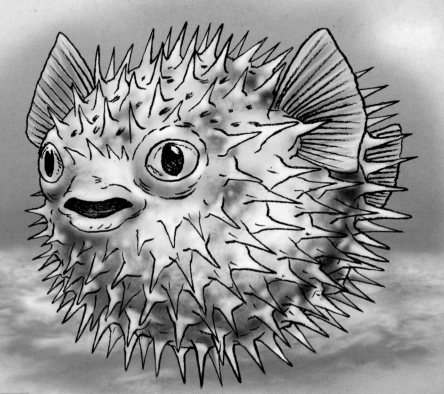

FINISHED!

# PURPLE SEA STAR

STEP 1

STEP 2

STEP 3

A purple sea star usually has five arms, but other species of sea stars have as many as 40 arms! A purple sea star feeds on mussels, barnacles, and snails. It does this by prying open the shells with its surprisingly strong arms. Then it inserts its stomach inside the shell to eat the prey. After its meal the sea star pulls its stomach back into its body.

STEP 4

FINISHED!

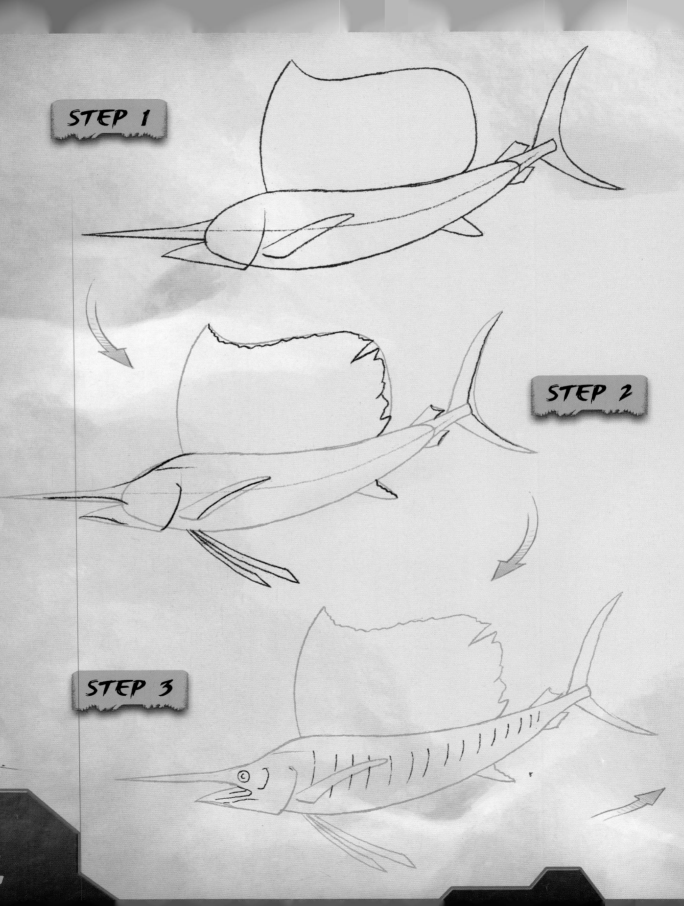

STEP 1

STEP 2

STEP 3

This amazing fish got its name from the large, dorsal fin that sticks up from its back. It also has a long, spearlike bill extending from its upper jaw that it may use to stun its prey. Perhaps most impressive is this fish's speed—it can leap out of the water at 68 miles (109 km) per hour.

**STEP 4**

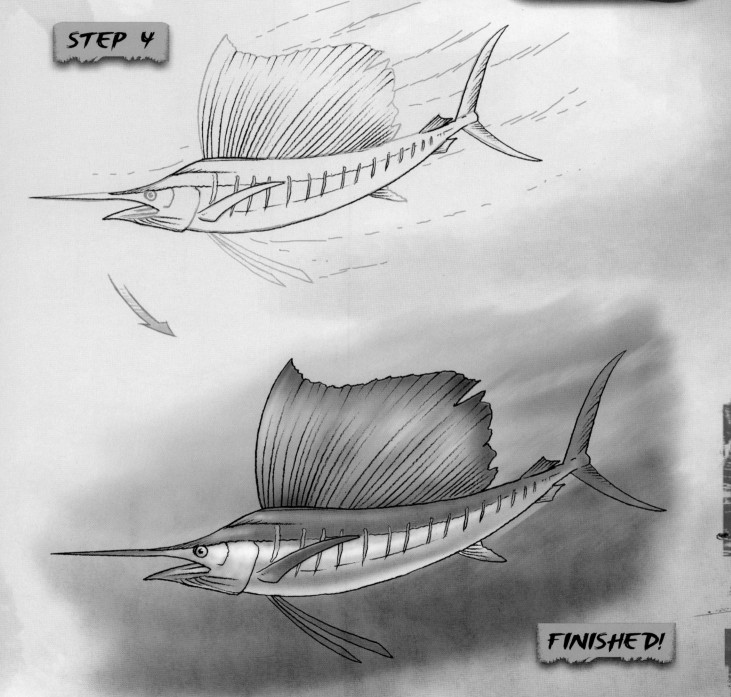

**FINISHED!**

Sea otters have the thickest fur of any mammal. Long guard hairs and a dense undercoat trap a layer of air that keeps them warm. Sea otters spend nearly all their time at sea. They float on their backs and use their stomachs as a table. They crack open clam and mussel shells using rocks.

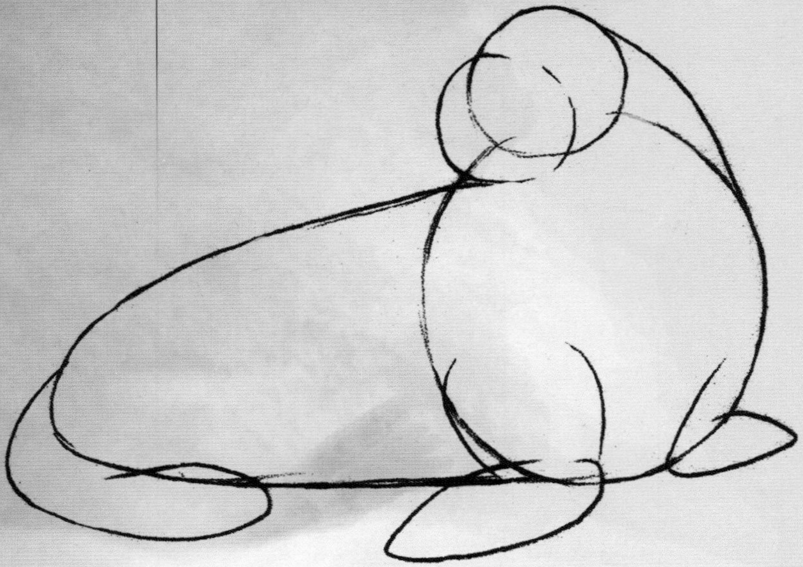

STEP 1

STEP 2

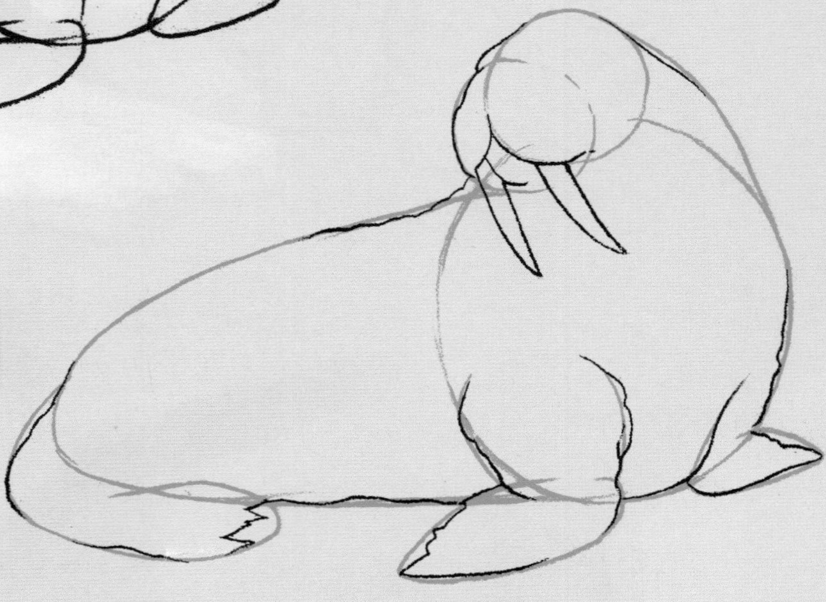

STEP 3

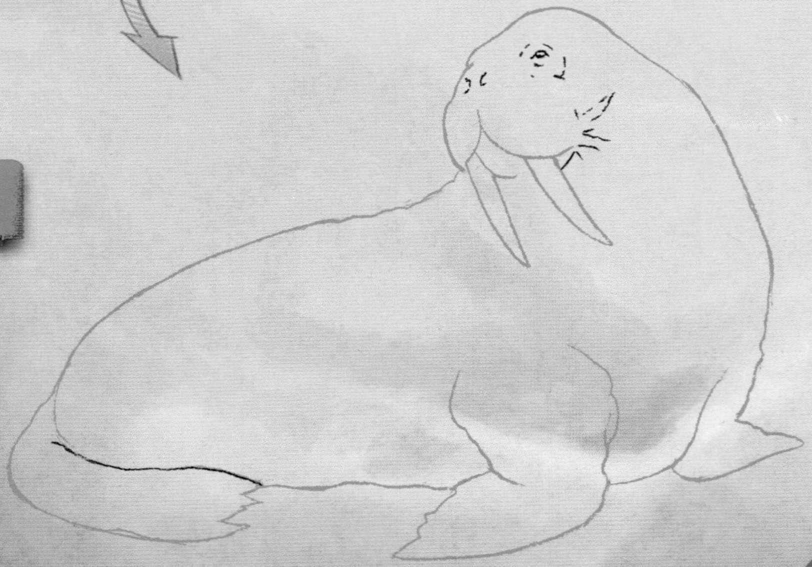

Walruses are perfectly suited for their arctic home. Blubber keeps them warm, and they can slow their heartbeats to help withstand the cold. Their large tusks look awkward, but they are helpful in climbing out of the water. They also use their tusks to break through ice to make breathing holes while under water.

STEP 4

FINISHED!

STEP 1

STEP 2

STEP 3

The wandering albatross, also called the snowy albatross, wins the record for longest wingspan of any bird at 11 feet (3.4 m). That's about twice the length of an adult human. This seabird uses its long wings to catch updrafts of wind over the ocean. It may soar for hours without flapping its wings.

STEP 4

FINISHED!

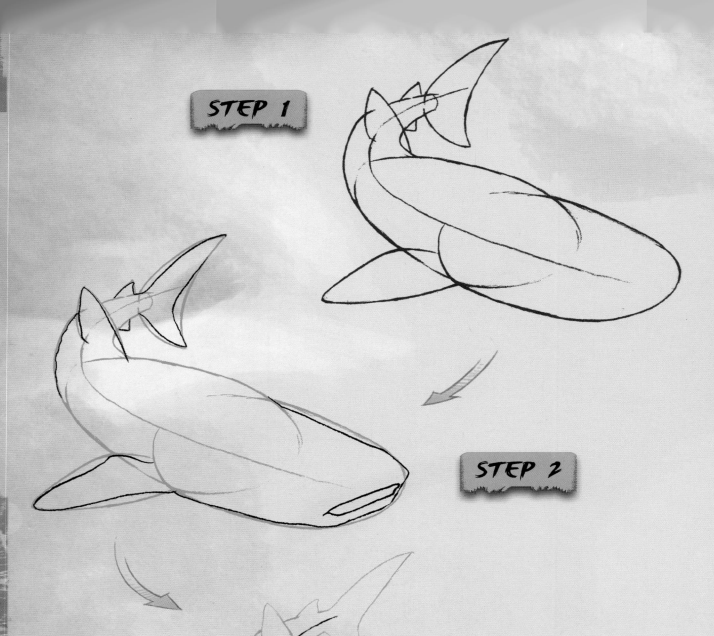

STEP 1

STEP 2

STEP 3

As the largest fish in the ocean, the whale shark could probably eat whatever it wants. But it prefers tiny plankton. The sharks take a large amount of water into their mouths, along with whatever plankton is in the water. Then they push the water out through their gills, keeping the plankton and eating it.

STEP 4

FINISHED!

# YETI CRAB

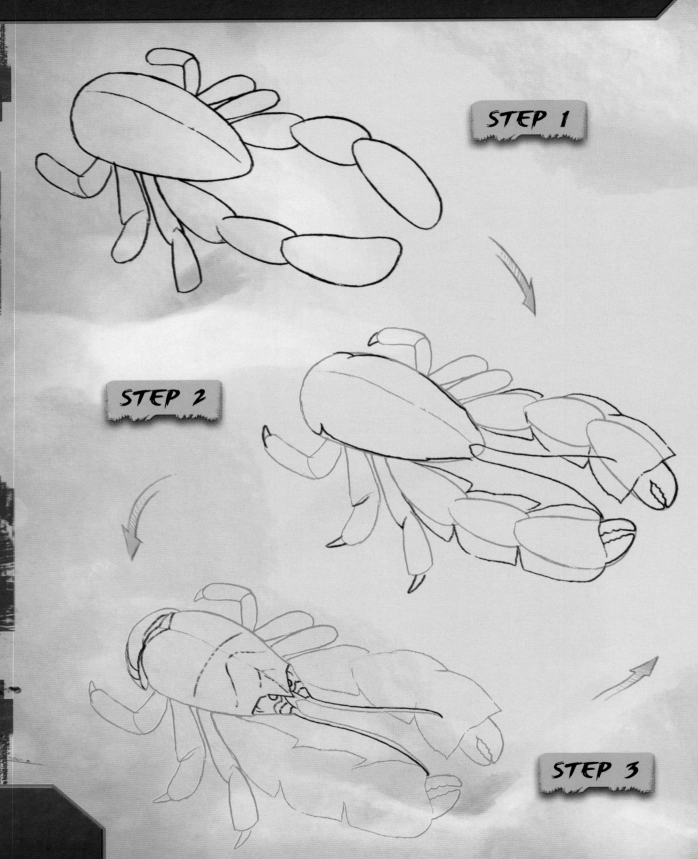

STEP 1

STEP 2

STEP 3

Living a mile or more below the surface of the ocean, these deep-sea creatures are used to life in the dark. Yeti crabs can't see, but they don't need to hunt anyway—yetis grow their own food on their hairy arms! Bacteria collect in the arm hairs. The crabs scrape the bacteria off with their mouths and eat them.

STEP 4

FINISHED!

Capstone Press
1710 Roe Crest Drive
North Mankato, Minnesota 56003
www.capstonepub.com

Library of Congress Cataloging-in-Publication Data
McCurry, Kristen.
  How to draw incredible ocean animals / by Kristen McCurry ;
illustrations by Jared Osterhold.
     pages cm. — (Smithsonian drawing books)
  Summary: "Provides information and step-by-step drawing
instructions for 30 ocean animals"—Provided by publisher.
  ISBN 978-1-4296-9940-2 (library binding)
  ISBN 978-1-62065-728-7 (paperback)
1.  Marine animals in art—Juvenile literature. 2.  Drawing—
Technique—Juvenile literature.  I. Osterhold, Jared, illustrator.
II. Title.
NC781.M39 2013
  743.6—dc23                    2012029957

**Editorial Credits:**

Kristen Mohn, editor
Alison Thiele, designer
Nathan Gassman, art director
Eric Gohl, media researcher
Kathy McColley, production specialist

Our very special thanks to Nancy Knowlton, Sant Chair of
Marine Sciences, National Museum of Natural History, for her
curatorial review. Capstone would also like to thank Ellen
Nanney and Kealy Wilson at the Smithsonian Institution's
Office of Licensing for their help in the creation of this book.

Smithsonian Enterprises: Carol LeBlanc, Vice President; Brigid
Ferraro, Director of Licensing

**Photo credits:**

Alamy: Stephen Frink Collection, 7; AP Images: Ifremer, A.
Fifis, 63; Corbis: Hoberman Collection, 17; iStockphotos:
Amanda Cotton, 53; Newscom: Getty Images/AFP/Justin
Marshall, 19, Zuma Press, 11; NOAA: Estuarine Research
Reserve Collection, 55; Shutterstock: A Cotton Photo, 39, Brian
Lasenby, 21, 31, Daleen Loest, 15, Darren J. Bradley, 51, Dray
van Beeck, 49 (bottom), Hiroshi Sato, 13, holbox, 9, Krzysztof
Odziomek, 61, Rich Carey, 27, Ryan M. Bolton, 43, Matt Reston,
49 (top), Satin, 33, stockpix4u, 5, Tatiana Ivkovich, 47, Tony
Wear, 35, totophotos, 41; Wikipedia: Albert Kok, 23, Barry
Peters, 29, Christian Mehlführer, 37, JJ Harrison, 59, National
Institute of Standards and Technology/Glenn Williams, 45,
Pterantula, 25, U.S. Fish and Wildlife Service, 57

# INTERNET SITES

FactHound offers a safe, fun way to find Internet sites
related to this book. All sites on FactHound have been
researched by our staff.

Here's all you do:

Visit www.facthound.com

Type in this code: 9781429699402

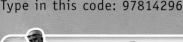

Check out projects, games and lots more at
www.capstonekids.com

Printed in the United States of America in North Mankato, Minnesota.
092012        006933CGS13